RAINER'S ACOUSTIC BLUES GUITAR PICKING SCHOOL

BY RAINER BRUNN

T0086977

Video Editor: Adam Traum

To access video visit:
www.halleonard.com/mylibrary

Enter Code
4585-7542-2378-6575

ISBN 978-1-70512-798-8

Visit Hal Leonard Online at
www.halleonard.com

Contact us:
Hal Leonard
7777 West Bluemound Road
Milwaukee, WI 53213
Email: info@halleonard.com

In Europe, contact:
Hal Leonard Europe Limited
42 Wigmore Street
Marylebone, London, W1U 2RN
Email: info@halleonardeurope.com

In Australia, contact:
Hal Leonard Australia Pty. Ltd.
4 Lentara Court
Cheltenham, Victoria, 3192 Australia
Email: info@halleonard.com.au

Contents

Introduction ▶

Hi Fellow Pickers,

Looking back to the days when I began playing blues music, I see a young fellow playing Bob Dylan songs and other folk stuff with the knowledge of just a few ordinary chords. One day, I was given a blues sampler album and, for the first time, I listened to the music of guys like Blind Blake, Tampa Red, Lightnin' Hopkins, and other fellows playing a kind of music I had never heard before.

Straight away, I tried to play this kind of music—and miserably failed! Of course, I failed because all I knew was strumming and a few standard chords.

I quickly forgot about this and started playing classical guitar before I got teased by blues music again. And, with a wider background of playing techniques, I felt this time I might succeed. If I'd had a method on basic blues picking at the time, I probably would not have started playing classical music (which I never regret) and would certainly have stuck with the blues.

After having published some video tutorials with HOMESPUN, I thought it might be a humble tribute to the blues if I wrote a method on how to get your blues picking started. Happy Traum encouraged me and supported my work in his usual friendly and confident manner, and so I am excited to present *Rainer's Acoustic Blues Guitar Picking School* through HOMESPUN.

I hope this will contribute to keeping this fantastic music alive and to knock over the hurdles that usually have to be jumped over whenever we begin to do something new.

And now, get started… and have fun!

Yours sincerely,
Rainer

About the Video Lessons

To download or stream the accompanying video lessons, simply visit *www.halleonard.com/mylibrary* and enter the code from page 1 of this book. Video icons ▶ appear throughout the book to indicate the sections with corresponding videos.

CHAPTER ONE

1.1. Thumb Picking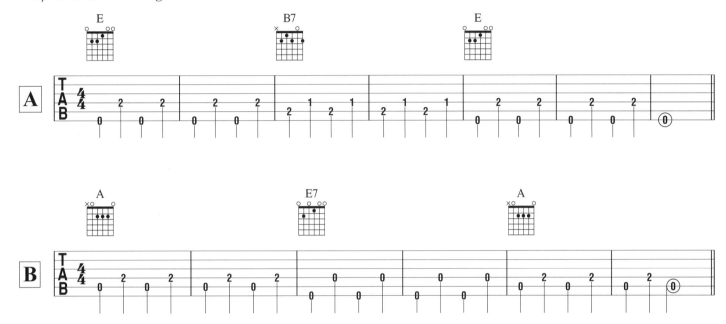

First, try to get that "muffled" bass-string sound by placing the palm of your right hand on top of the bass strings very close to the bridge!

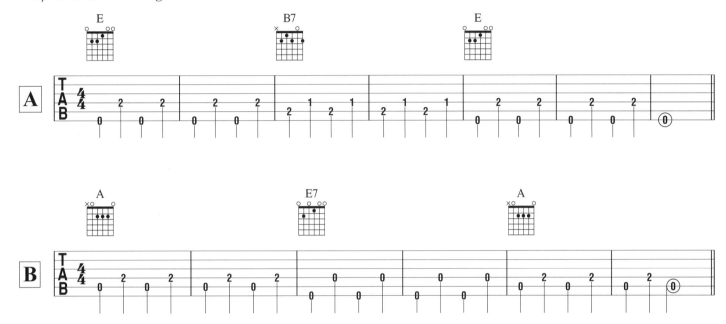

1.2. Adding Right-Hand Fingers ▶

Let's add the right-hand fingers now!

Advice: Use three fingers for your picking—index finger (i), middle finger (m), and ring finger (r). Once you have become familiar with this technique, it will make everything much more comfortable.

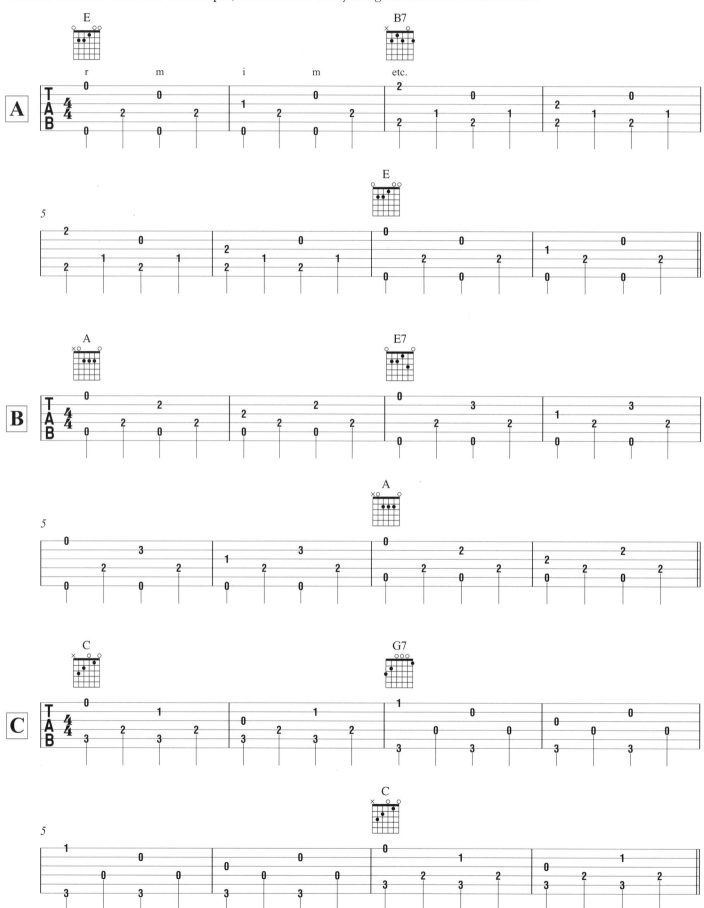

1.3. Syncopations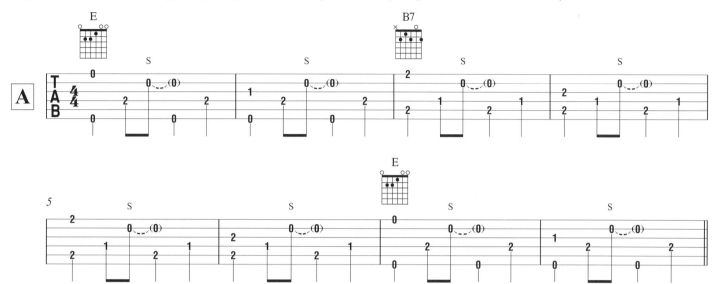

You say this didn't sound bluesy at all? You're right! To make it sound a little bluesy, we can insert some syncopations. That means we play some of the finger notes *before* we play the bass notes! Syncopations are the rhythmic key to blues, ragtime, and jazz! In example A, all syncopations are indicated by "S."

When two notes are combined by a tie, it means that you only hold the notes for their combined length; don't play the second note.

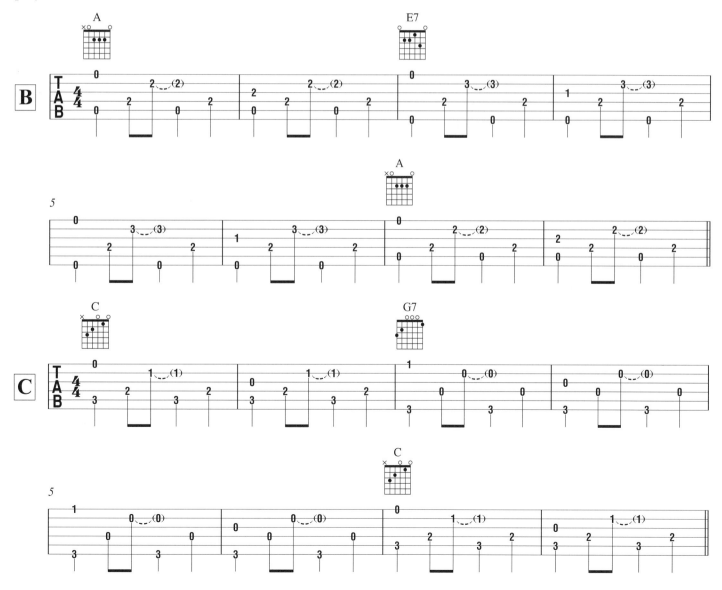

1.4. Other Syncopations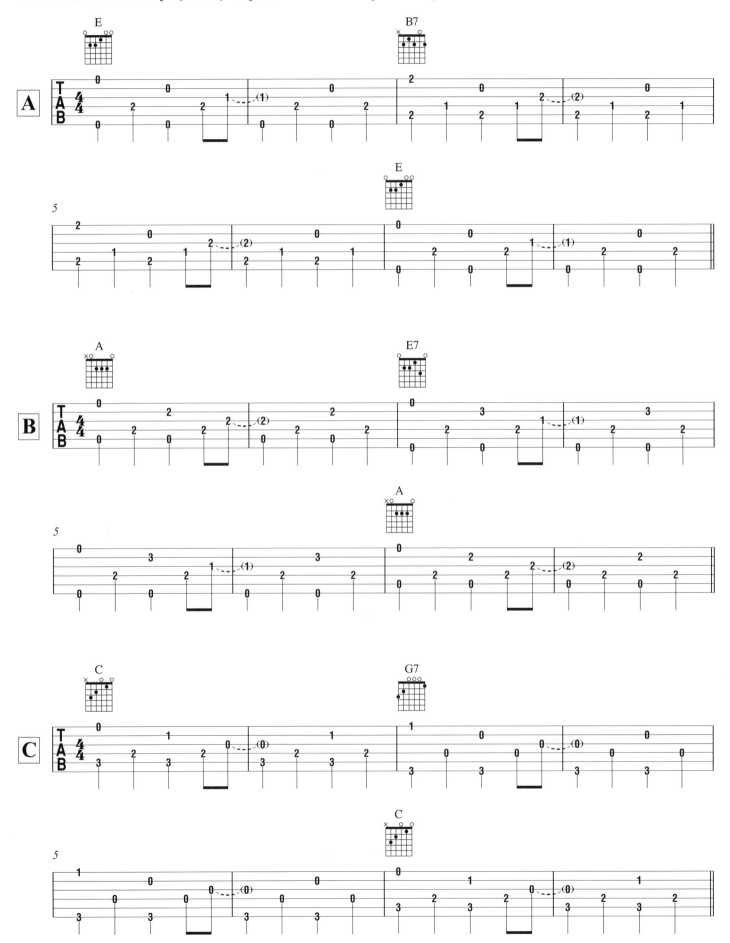

Of course, we can also play the syncopations in different places! Try this!

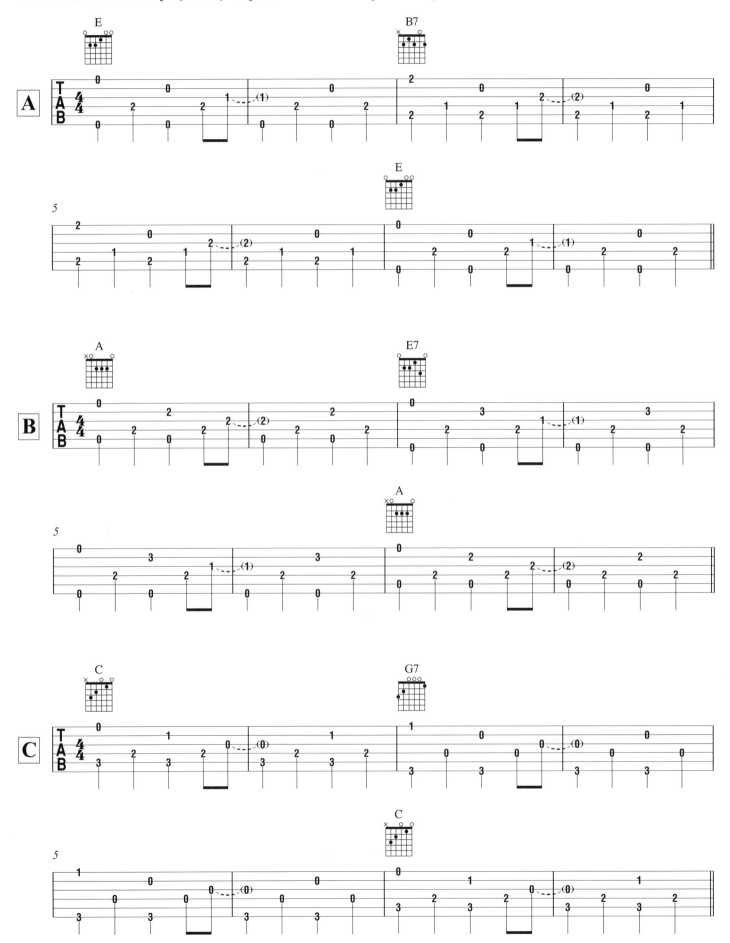

1.5. Additional Melodic Notes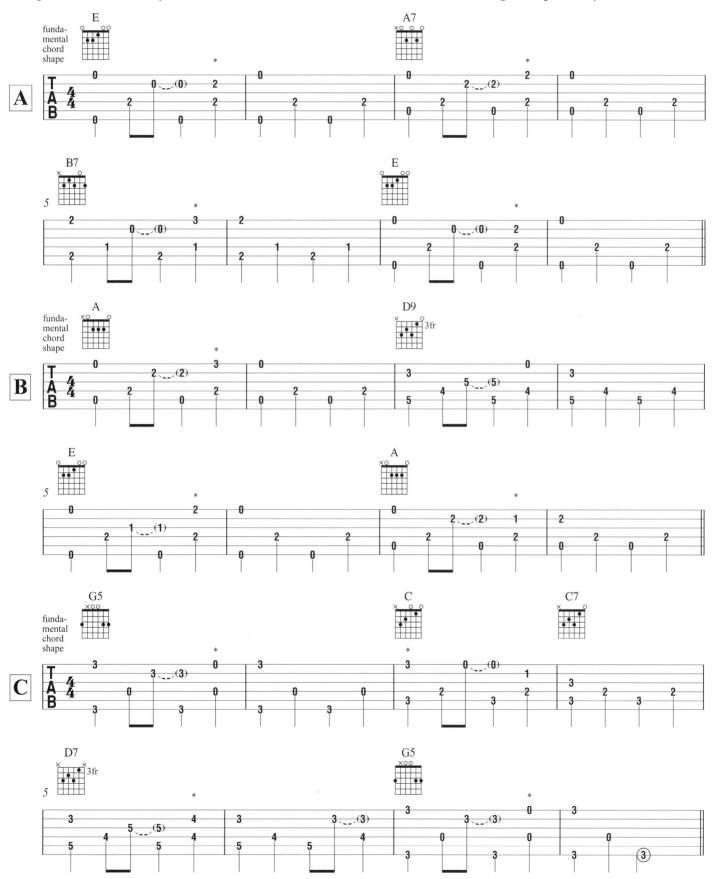

Let's try to bring in some additional melodic notes. That's very often the task of our pinky finger! I've written "fundamental chord shapes" on my tabs. These are normal chord shapes to which, in certain places, we either add a finger or take one away! Additional notes are marked with * (in the following examples only).

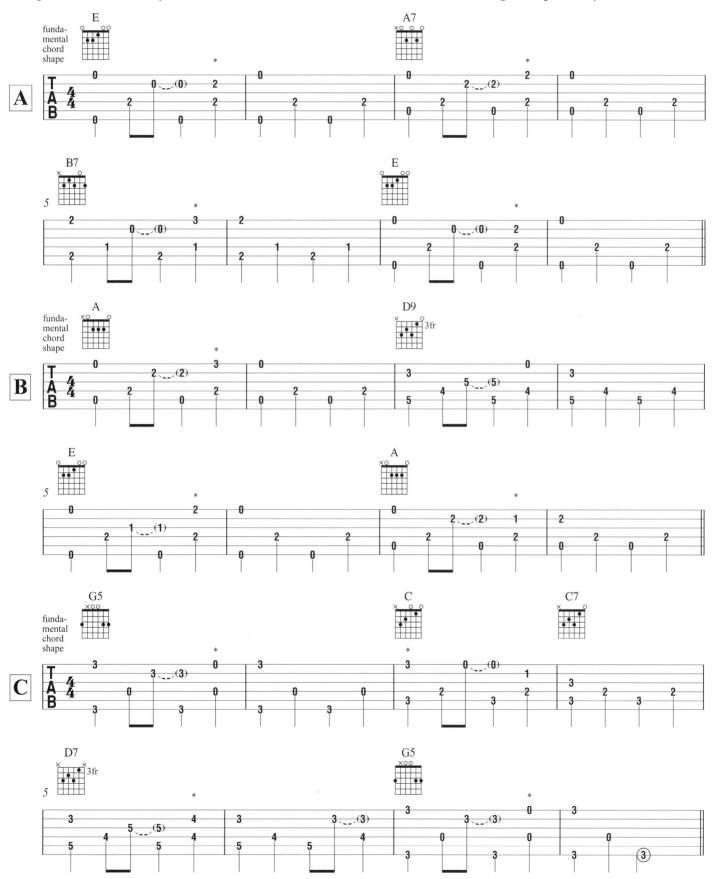

1.6. First Solo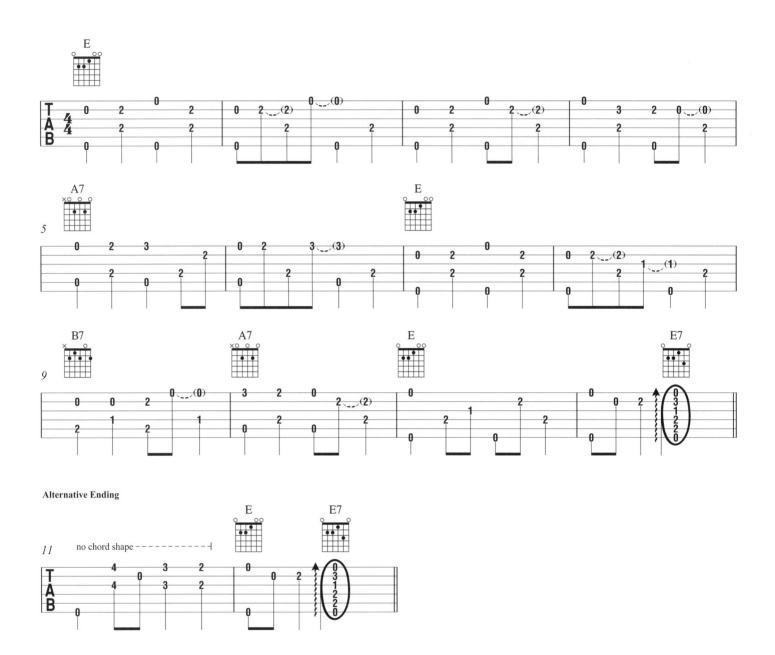

For this little 12-bar blues solo, I suggest we use our right-hand technique and assign a certain finger to a certain string—index for 3rd string, middle finger for 2nd string, and ring finger for 1st string.

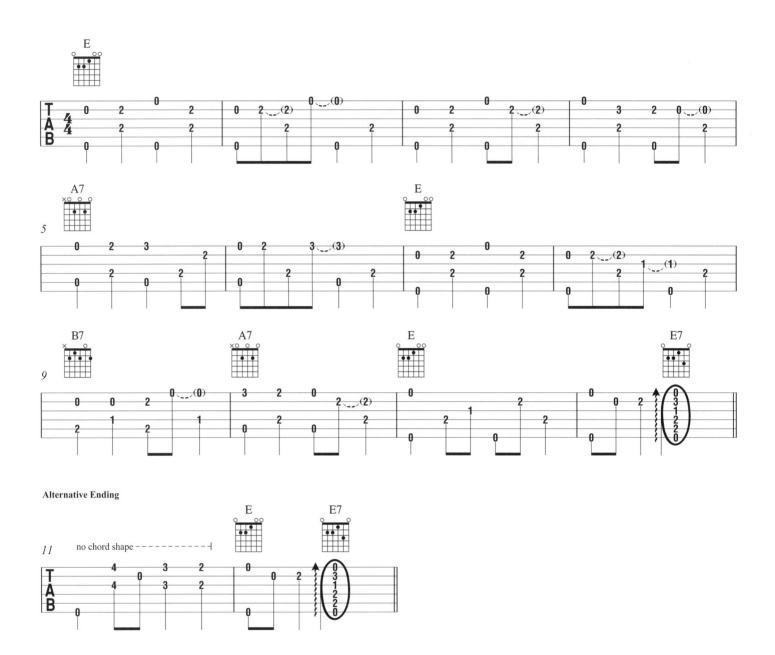

1.7. Picking Nerd's Supplies for Chapter One

In the following song, I play with a "swinging 8ths" or "shuffled" rhythmic style. Watch the video to hear what this sounds like. You'll learn more about the shuffle in Chapter Five.

"Joshua Fit the Battle of Jericho"

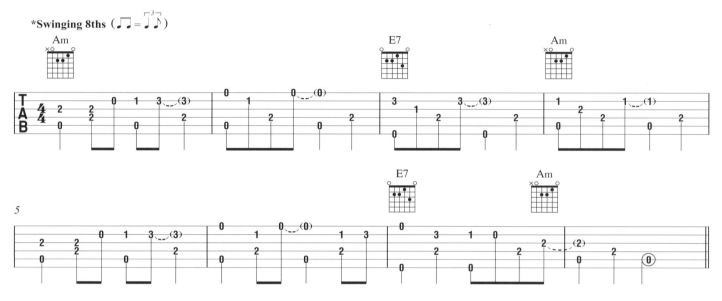

*Shuffle Rhythm: see Chapter 5 for more about this.

Rainer's Blues School Advice 1

CHAPTER TWO

2.1. Inner and Outer Right-Hand Positions

In Chapter One, we learned the assignment of certain strings. We played:

- the 3rd string with the index finger
- the 2nd string with the middle finger
- the 1st string with the ring finger

Let's call this the "inner position." Whenever we play a chord that leaves out the 5th and 6th strings—for example D, D minor, or the "small F" chord—our thumb will use the G string for alternating bass notes. This means we have to move to the "outer position," in which our index finger now plays the 2nd string, and our middle finger plays the 1st string. Our ring finger is unemployed for a while! This might need a little practice!

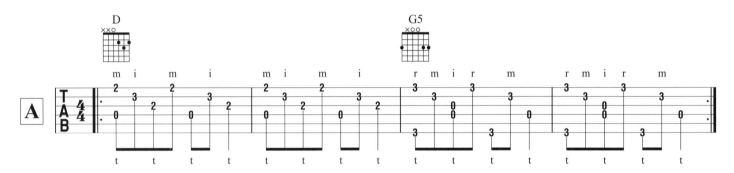

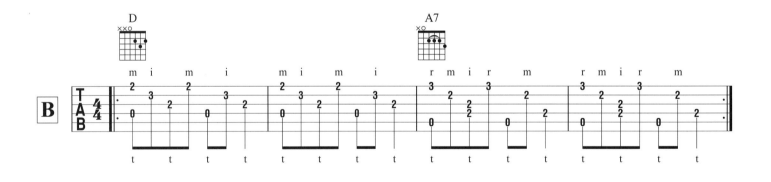

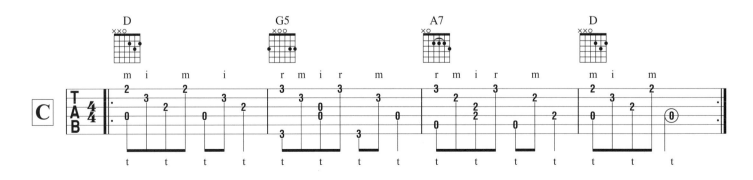

2.2. Easy Backup for "Stealin'"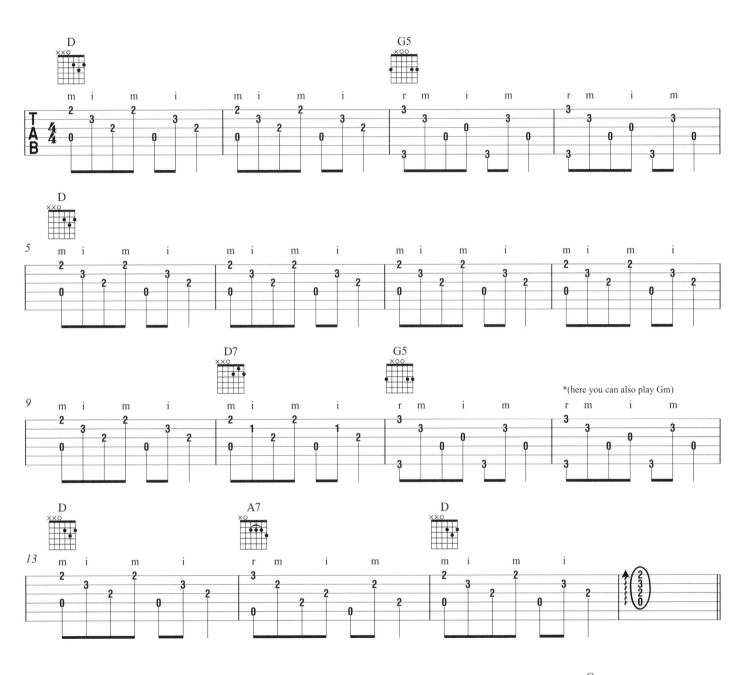

Here's an easy backup for the famous song "Stealin'," originally played by the Memphis Jug Band. In this backup, we can practice the changing of the right-hand finger positions. All D bars use outer position, and all other bars use inner position.

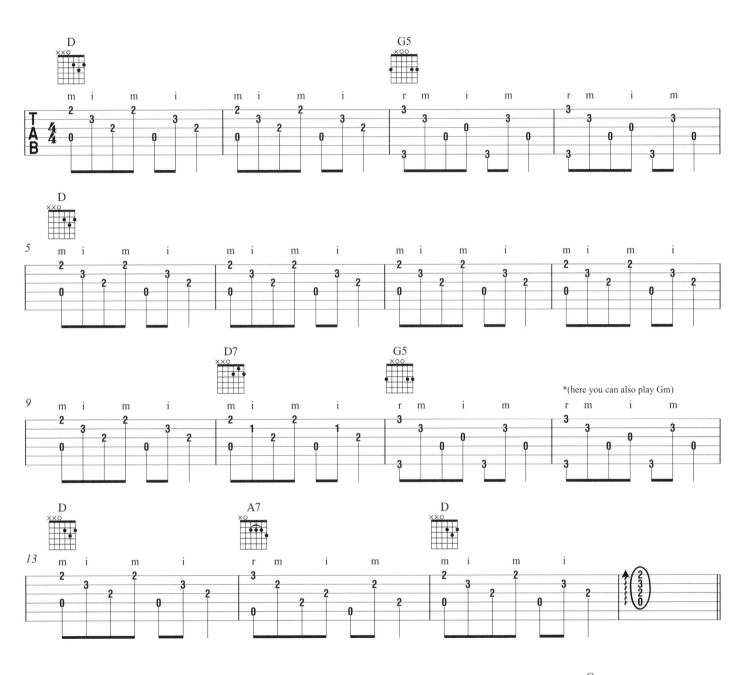

*If you are familiar with the G minor chord, you can use it in bar 12 instead of G major:

2.3. Picking Nerd's Supplies for Chapter Two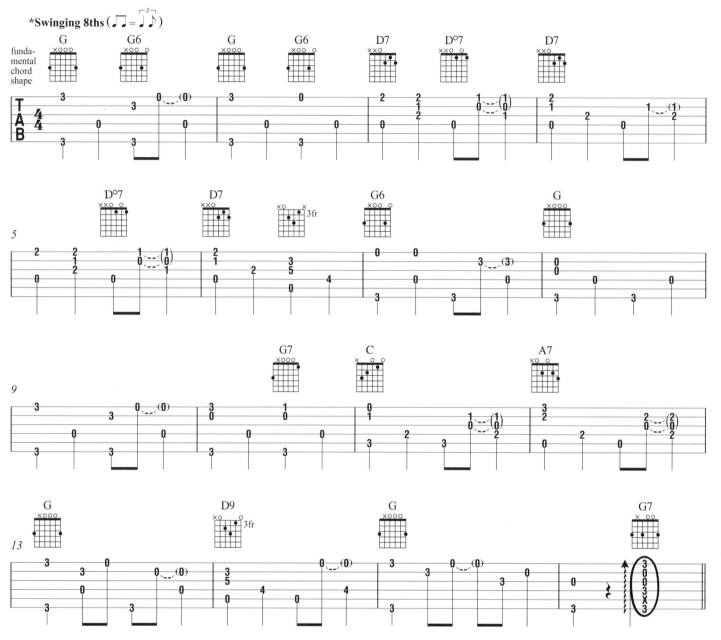

*Shuffle Rhythm: see Chapter 5 for more about this.

▶ **Rainer's Blues School Advice 2**

CHAPTER THREE

3.1. The "Long" A Chord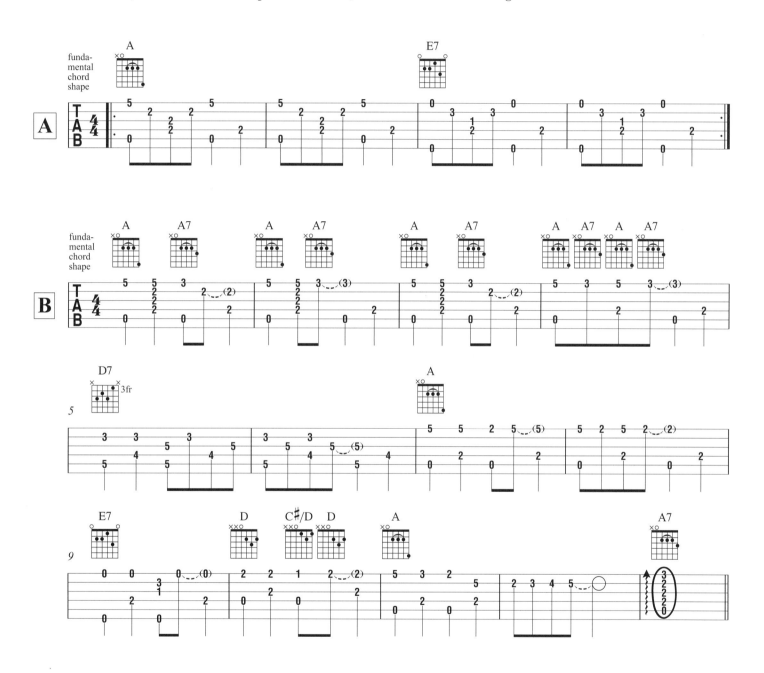

In this exercise, we learn a new A-position chord, which is called the "long" A chord.

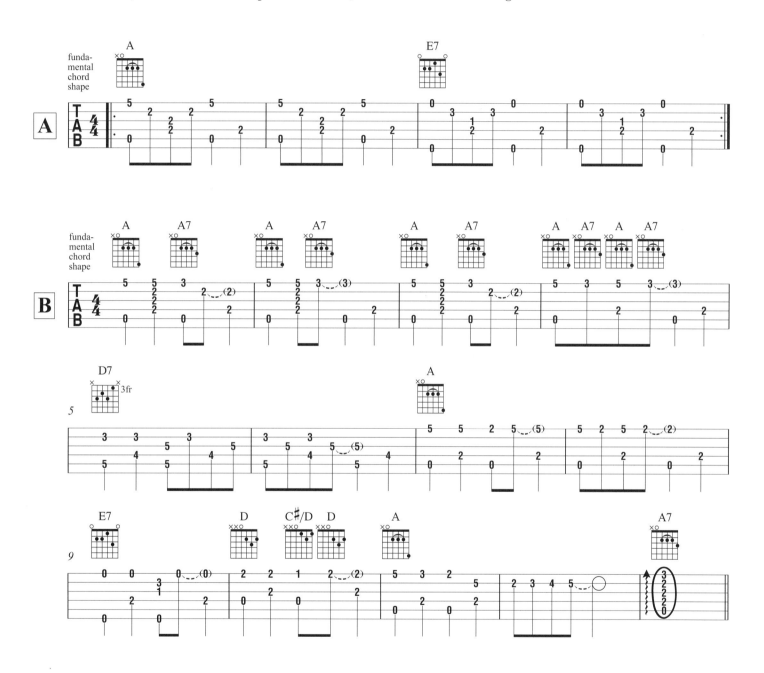

3.2. Another Solo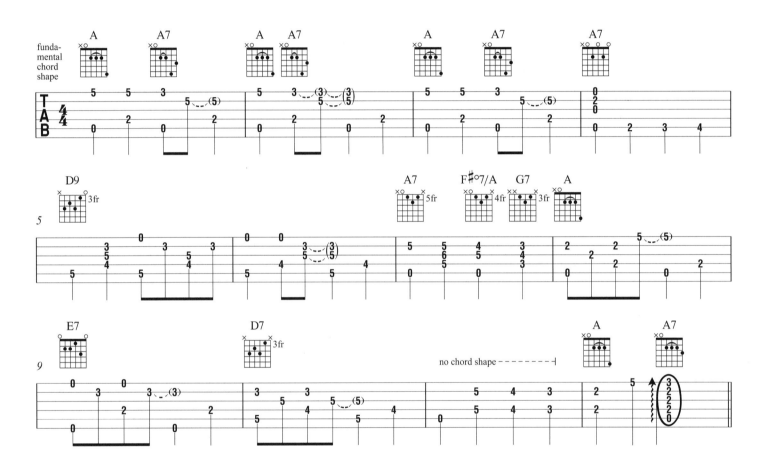

Here's another little blues solo, this time in the key of A. We can play this one completely out of the inner right-hand position:

- 3rd string – index finger

- 2nd string – middle finger

- 1st string – ring finger

There's a new A7 chord shape in the second position occurring in bars 1–3. And still another new A7 chord position in bar 7, which we then just move down fret by fret. Don't be scared by the names of the chords!

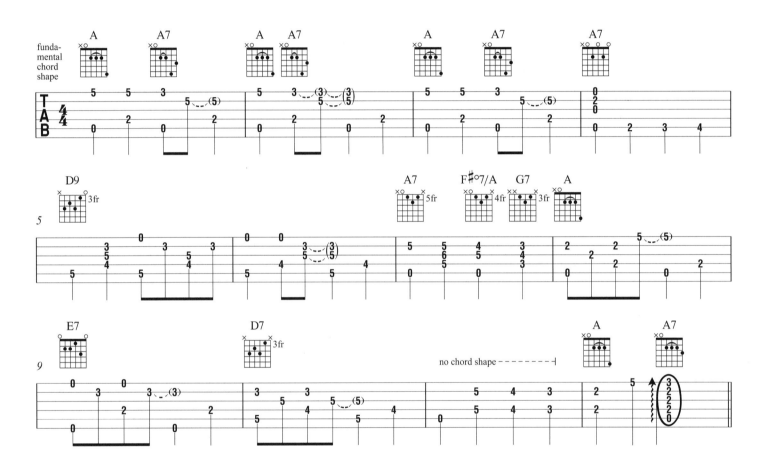

3.3. Same Solo with Double Alternating Bass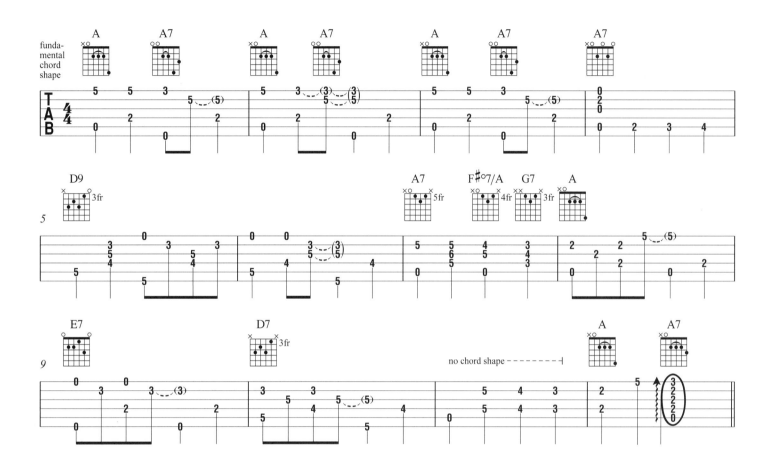

In this little variation, we have what I call "double alternating bass" in bars 1, 2, 3, 5, 6, and 10. That means that instead of repeating the basic note on beat 3, we choose a different chord note for the thumb! So look out for every third beat in the mentioned bars!

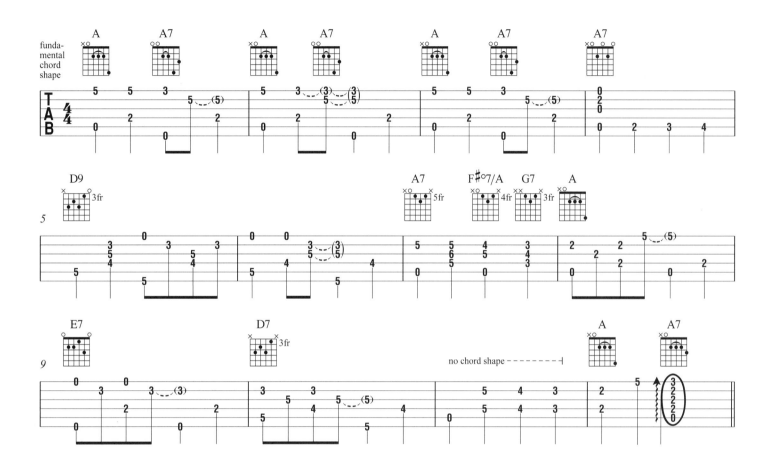

CHAPTER FOUR

4.1. Hammer-Ons, Pull-Offs, and Slides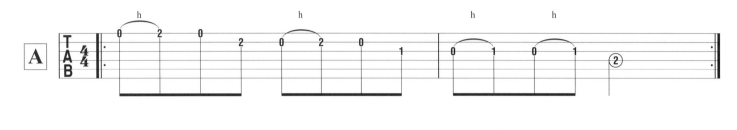

Let's practice three essential guitar techniques: hammer-ons (h), pull-offs (p), and slides (sl).

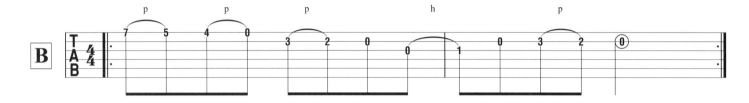

Take your time practicing the next two examples and play them until you feel very comfortable with them!

In the following example, we have some triplets. That means we divide one beat into *three* notes instead of two! What's also new here is that our slides are played as grace notes.

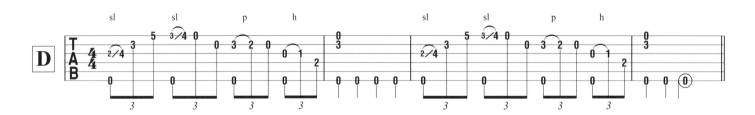

4.2. Tricky Solo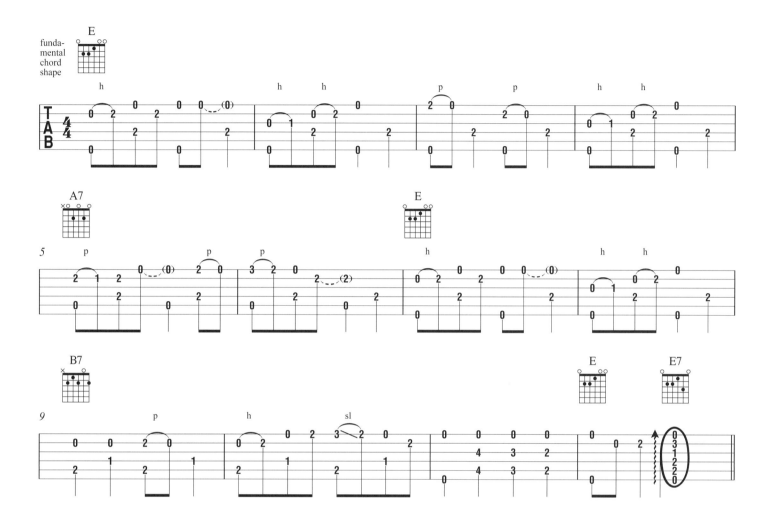

In this solo, we can really practice hammer-ons and pull-offs. And we have a nice turnaround in the ending! (You'll learn more about turnarounds later in the book.)

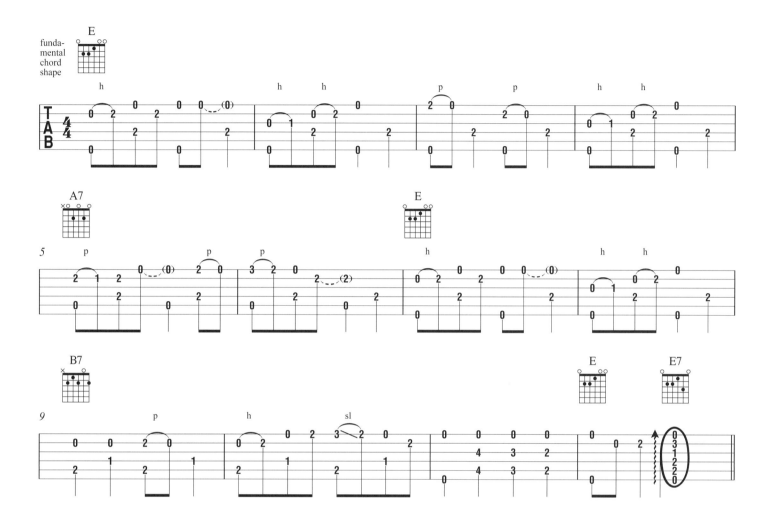

4.3. Picking Nerd's Supplies for Chapter Four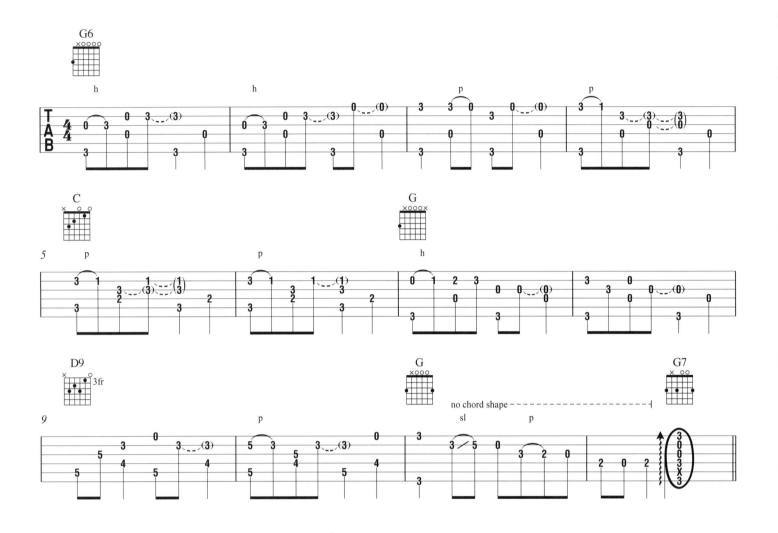

4.4. Picking Nerd's Extra Supplies for Chapter Four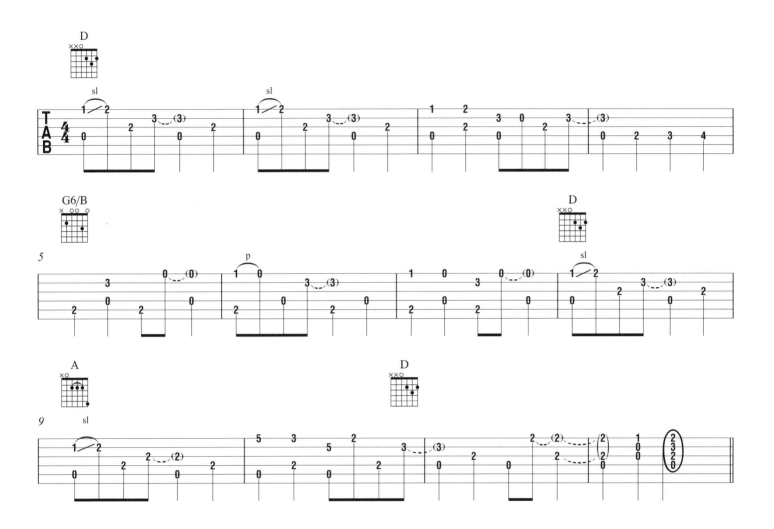

"Stagger Lee"

CHAPTER FIVE

5.1. Shuffle Rhythm

In blues and swing music, we often play a so-called "shuffle" rhythm, which means that we play swinging 8th notes. You already heard me play with a shuffle rhythm in some of the "Picking Nerd's Supplies" videos earlier in the book.

So when we read straight 8ths, like in bar 1, we play what is shown in bar 2 instead. Please listen to further explanations in the video! Note that when I say "fourth note" in the video, I mean "quarter note."

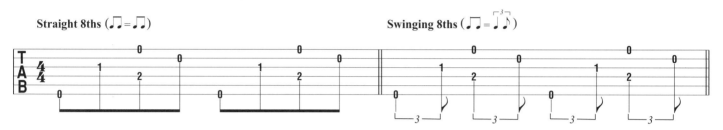

I always mark a shuffle rhythm by the note "Swinging 8ths" in the music notation.

5.2. Advanced Chord Shapes for the Key of E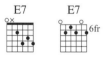

When we want to play higher melody notes in our solos, it becomes necessary to know various chord shapes of the chords we use. Let's start in the key of E.

We have two new E7 chord shapes:

And we have one new B7 shape:

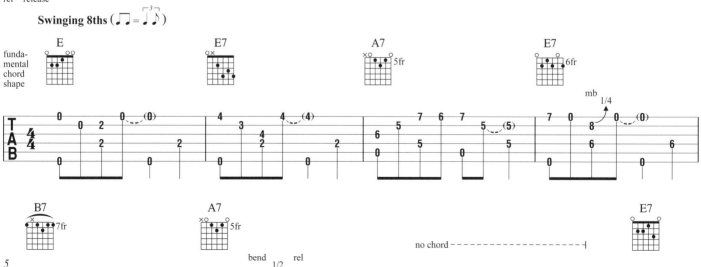

5.3. Advanced Chord Shapes
for the Key of A

In this exercise in the key of A, we learn some new A7 and D7 chord positions.

These are two A7 positions:

And here is a new D7 position:

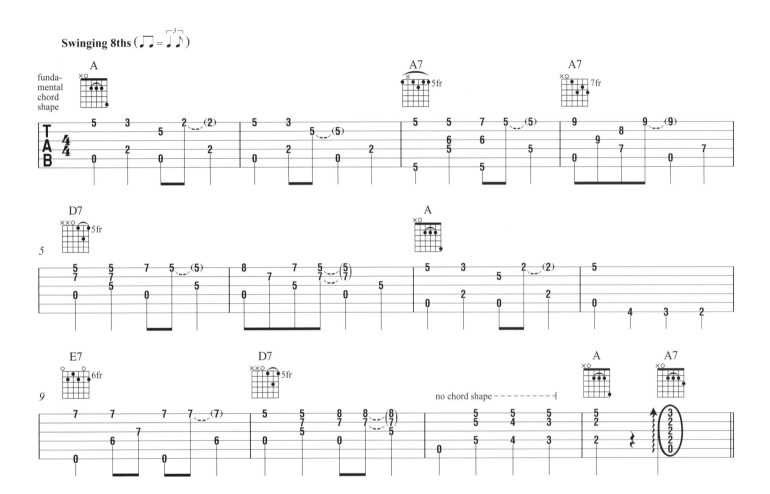

5.4. Advanced Chord Shapes for the Key of D

Drop D Tuning (DADGBE)

When we play blues in D, it's often better to tune the lower E string to D. We call that drop D tuning.

In this exercise, we again learn some new chord positions, but these are based on drop D tuning.

There are two new D shapes, as well as a D7 shape:

Plus, two new G7 shapes:

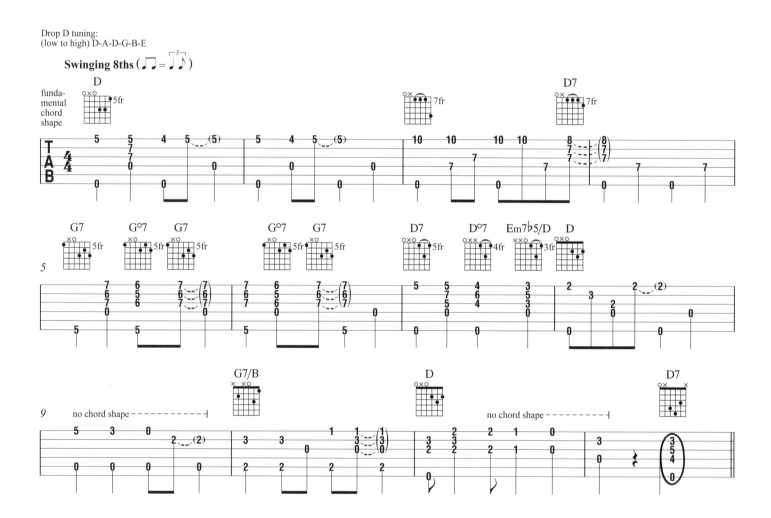

26

CHAPTER SIX

6.1. A Little Rag in C

In the key of C, there are not many effective higher chord positions, so we have to discuss a new technique: Fretting the 6th string with the thumb of your left hand! When you play a concert guitar, this will be very difficult because of the wider neck, but it's quite a common thing on steel-string and electric guitars. I have been educated in classical guitar, so I was not used to it when I started to play blues. But for one reason, I use this technique—thumb-fretting this special F chord:

F

T 321

It's basically a normal F chord, which you could also play as a barre chord, but I often want to play an additional D note in the melody using the 3rd fret of the B string. If we used a normal barre chord for this purpose, we must lift the pinky from the 4th string in order to play the desired D on the B string. But then we would get a 7th as the alternating bass note, which we don't want here. So, we are glad to use an F chord shape in which our thumb frets the 6th-string bass note.

Again, we have swinging 8ths in this song—a little ragtime in C with some new diminished chords.

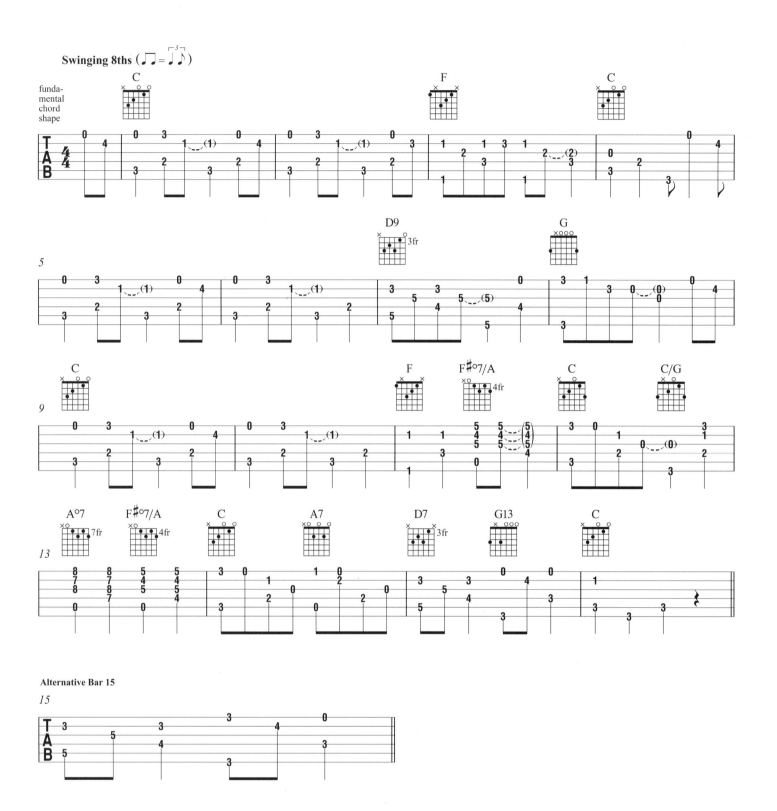

CHAPTER SEVEN

7.1. Combination of Hammers, Pulls, and Slides with Bass Notes

In this exercise, we want to practice combining hammer-ons, pull-offs, and slides with bass notes. We will play swinging 8ths.

Combination of hammer-on and bass note: We play the bass note at exactly the same moment the hammering finger hits the target fret!

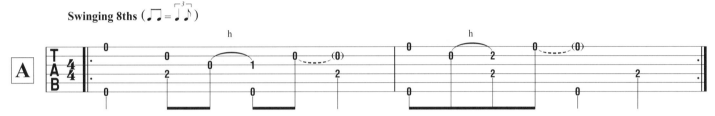

Combination of pull-off and bass note: We play the bass note exactly when the pulling finger "picks" the string!

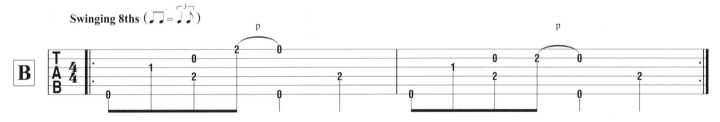

Combination of slide and bass note: We play the bass note when the sliding finger reaches the target fret!

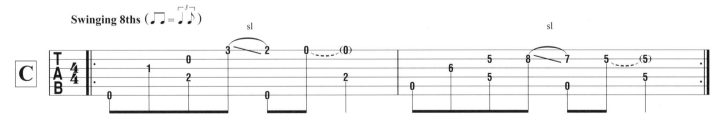

7.2. Another Tricky Solo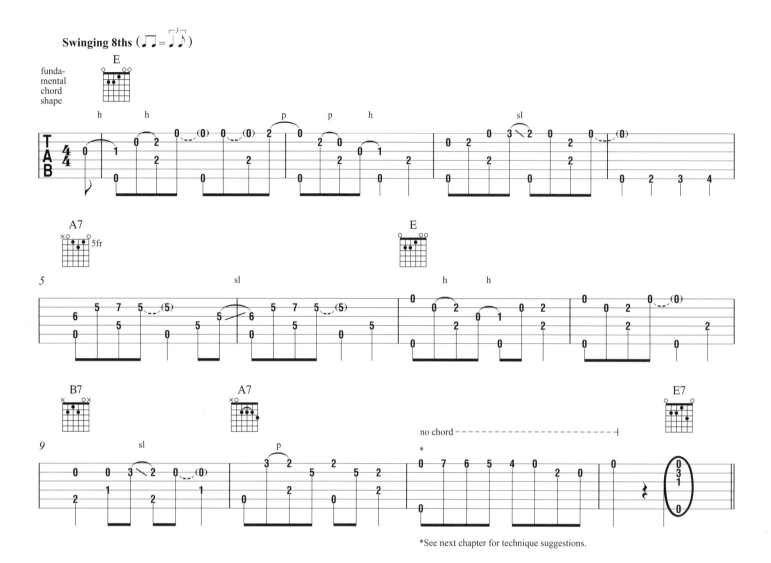

*See next chapter for technique suggestions.

7.3. Picking Nerd's Supplies for Chapter Seven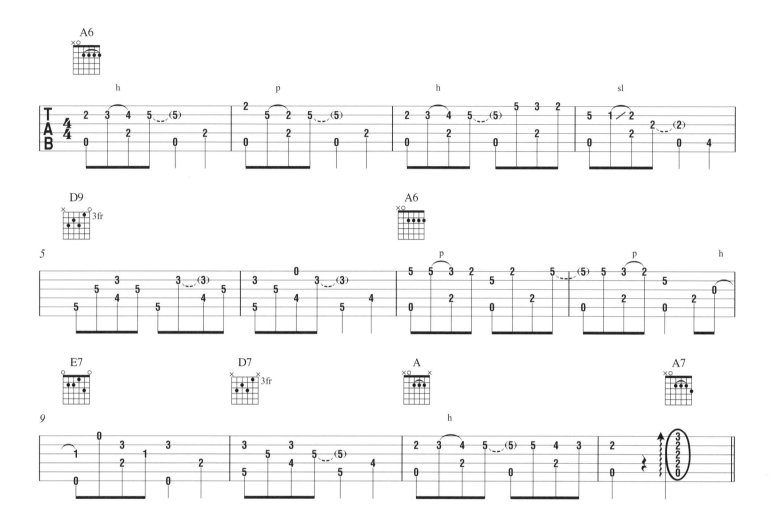

CHAPTER EIGHT

8.1. Melody Playing with Alternating Right-Hand Fingers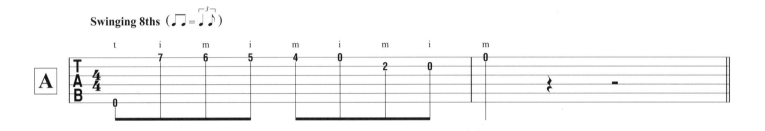

Let's have a look at the last two bars of Exercise 7.2. You have probably experienced that it can be very uncomfortable, if not impossible, to pick a row of numerous notes on one single string with one finger. There are two possibilities to make this easier.

The first option is an alternation of index finger and middle finger. This is what guitarists normally do. If you practice this for the first time, you will probably find it to be a little difficult. But from my experience, I know that students learn this technique rather quickly. Give it a try!

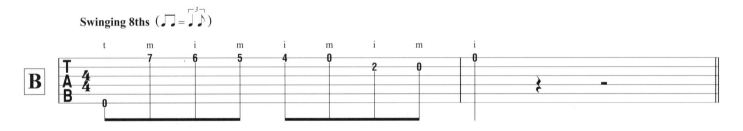

Or, in a different order:

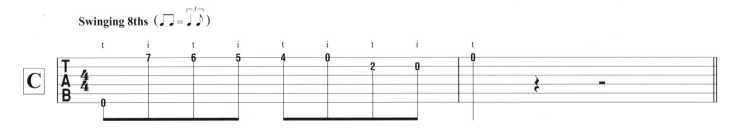

The second option is an alternation between thumb and index finger. That's what lute players do! A disadvantage of this technique is that you cannot use it when you want to keep the bass going!

8.2. Melody Playing over Bass Notes

Here we have an exercise in the key of E with steady, non-alternating bass under a single-note melody. When we play bass notes under our melodies, we don't have the option of playing the melody with the thumb and index finger, so we have to choose alternation between the index finger and middle finger. I will often use my ring finger in appropriate passages.

Please note that these suggestions are not rules. You will have to find your own way to play your music. Whatever sounds right is good, no matter how you do it.

Also, the term "position" occurs in this exercise. This always refers to the position of the 1st finger (index), whether it presses a string or not. So, the position that allows us to reach from the 1st to the 4th fret is called "1st position." When only my 4th finger (pinky) presses a certain string at the 4th fret, it is still in 1st position. Second position allows us to play from the 2nd to the 5th fret, etc.

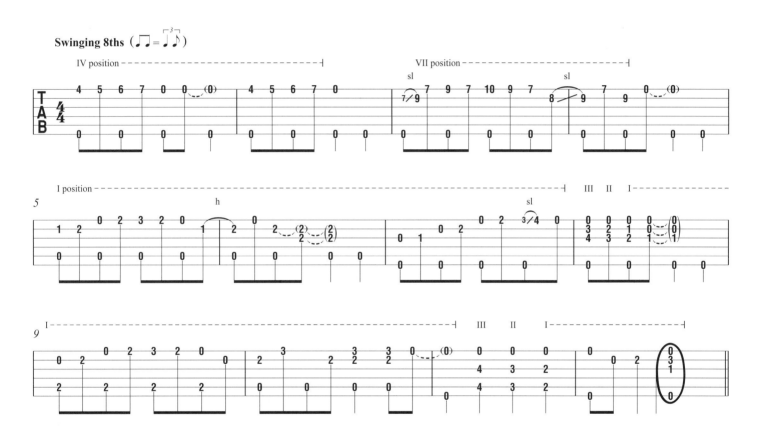

8.3. Another One with a Minor Feeling

Here is another example in the key of A with a minor feeling.

8.4. And Still Another One

And finally, here is another one—this time in the key of G.

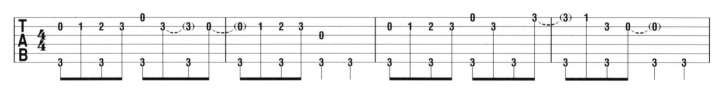

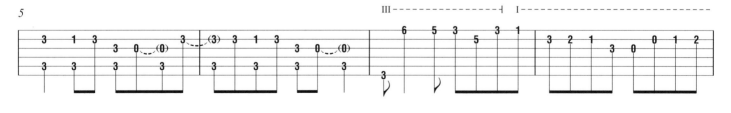

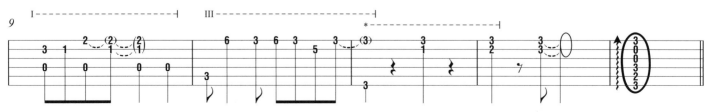

*These three notes should be played *staccato*,
which means very short (please watch video).

CHAPTER NINE

9.1. Backup for "Stagger Lee" ▶️

Backups should be designed simply and not too sophisticated. The singing is the important thing, and the audience should not be distracted from it by an overly conspicuous accompaniment.

As you follow the lyrics, you will notice that I have placed some syllables over unaccented notes in order to bring some syncopations into my singing!

Here's a suggested accompaniment to the famous folk-blues song "Stagger Lee":

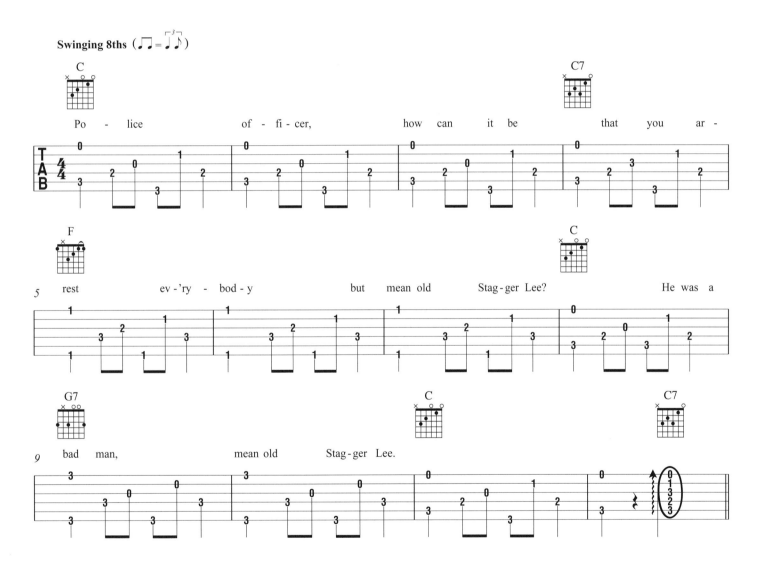

Studying this backup, you will have noticed that it follows a certain picking pattern! I find this works, and novices will welcome that, but as our playing and our taste become a bit more refined, we will increasingly find it boring to play the same pattern throughout a whole song. In the next exercise, I will show you how to vary patterns by changing just a few things!

9.2. Modifying a Backup Pattern

In the first two bars of each example, we have a basic idea for a backup. In bars 3 and 4, we have a slight variation. There are always a whole lot of possibilities to bring some diversity into our playing!

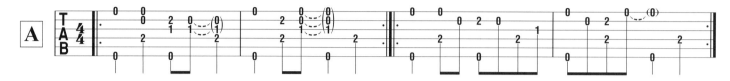

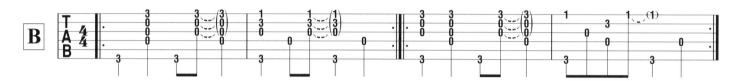

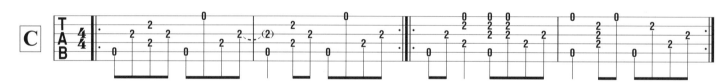

9.3. Boogie-Woogie-Like Rhythms

Here's a little boogie-woogie-like rhythm for different chords. The trick is to add the 6th of the respective basic chord! Again, we slightly change the pattern in the second half. At the left of each line, you'll find the fundamental chord shape to which we have to add one additional finger.

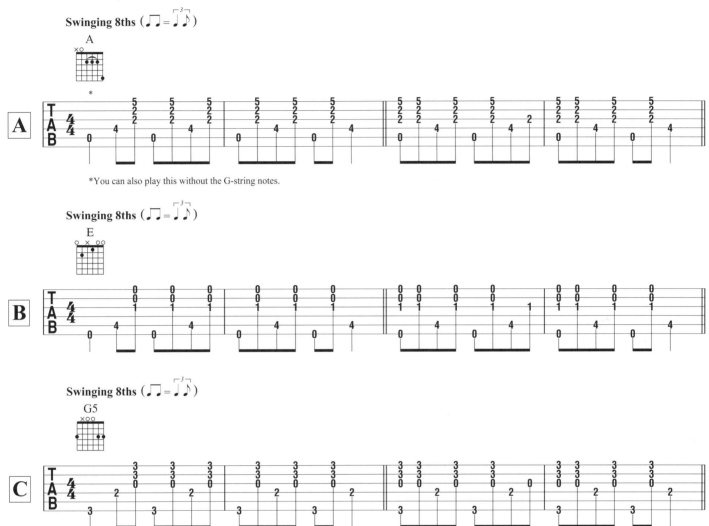

*You can also play this without the G-string notes.

In the following examples, the G string is played by the thumb.

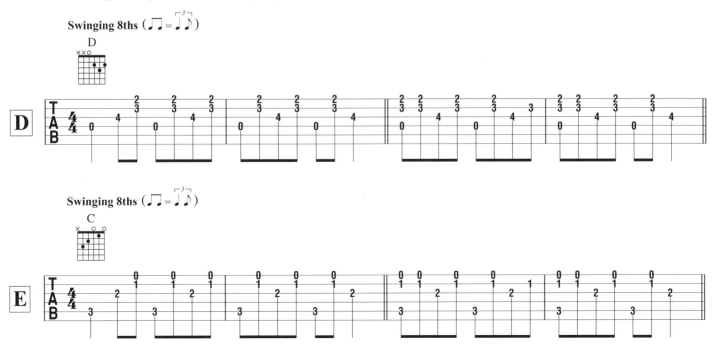

9.4. 12-Bar Boogie-Blues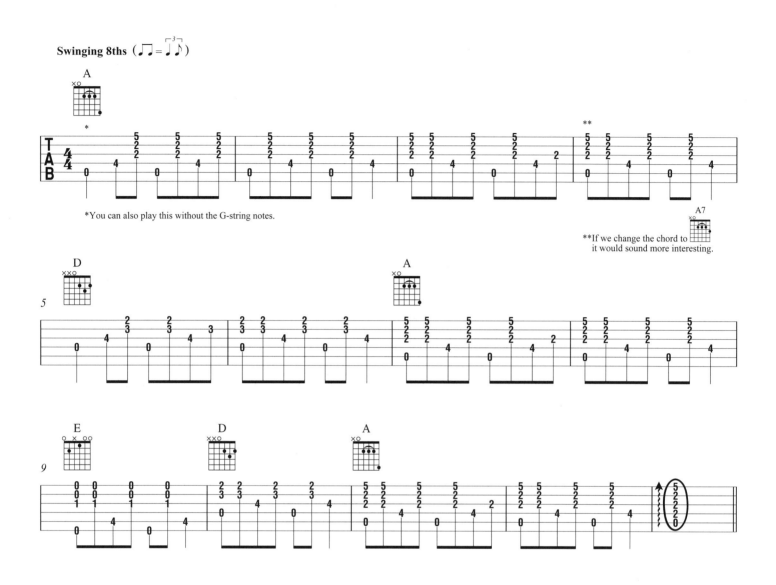

Now we can put some elements together to create a 12-bar boogie-blues.

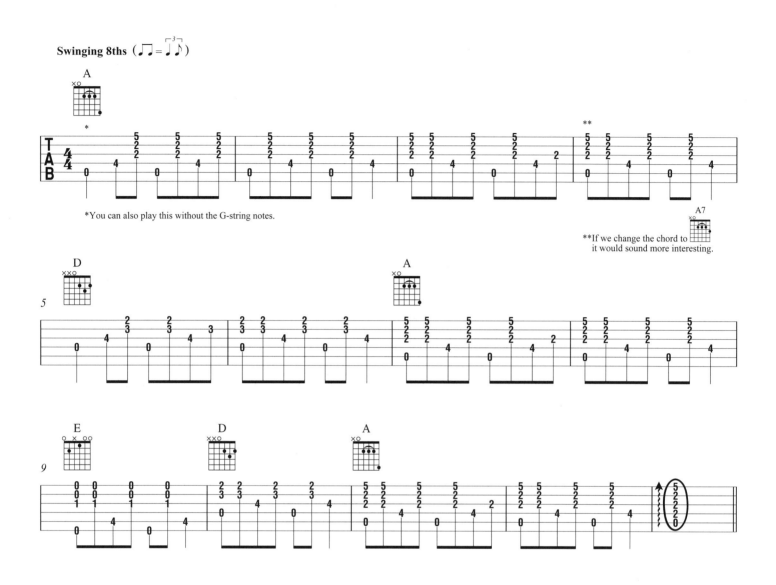

*You can also play this without the G-string notes.

**If we change the chord to A7
it would sound more interesting.

CHAPTER TEN

10.1. Moveable Stuff in the Key of E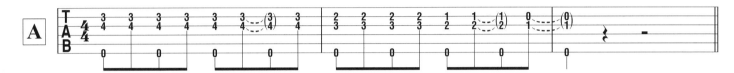

Good "modules," or elements, for solos are moveable 3rds, 6ths, and chords. You can use this stuff whenever you are on the basic chord of a certain key. Here's a little collection for the key of E. Of course, you can play all these examples with different rhythms (see next exercise), and you can play them in both directions!

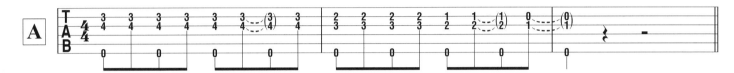

With additional notes on the 1st string:

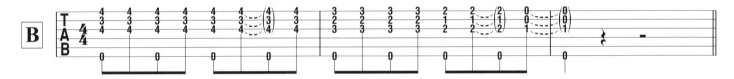

And the same in 6ths:

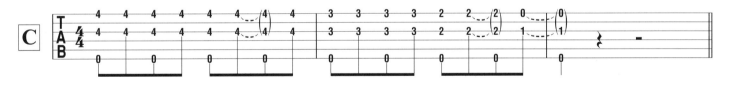

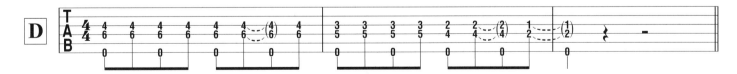

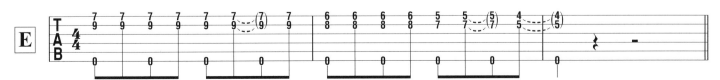

This one is the same as Example A, but played in 7th position:

The combination of Examples E and F:

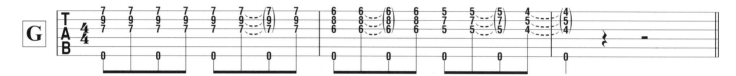

And the same in 6ths:

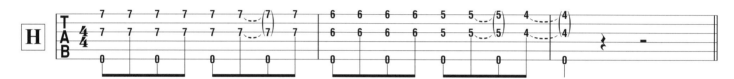

Important: You can take each example and move the first chord to positions back and forth! For example:

10.2. Moveable Stuff in the Key of A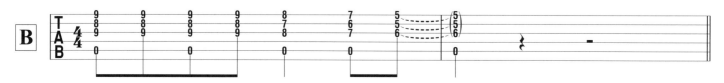

Here is some moveable stuff in the key of A, but this time in a different rhythmic context. You can use this collection whenever you are on the basic chord in the key of A.

With additional notes on the 1st string:

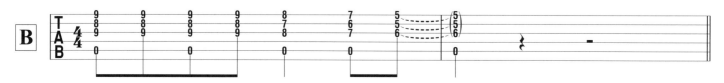

In 6ths:

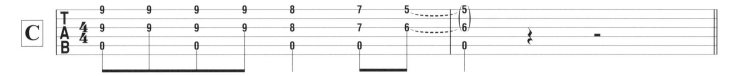

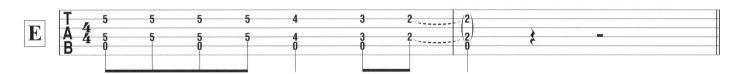

The same as Example D, one octave higher:

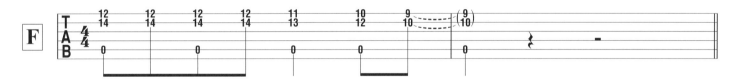

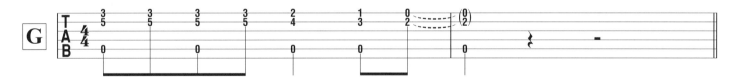

A combination of Examples D and G:

10.3. Moveable Stuff in the Key of D ▶️

Drop D Tuning (DADGBE)

Here's a collection for the key of D.

Drop D tuning:
(low to high) D-A-D-G-B-E

Swinging 8ths (♫ = ♩♪)

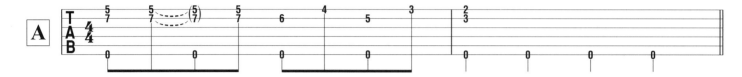

With additional notes on the 3rd string:

Drop D tuning:
(low to high) D-A-D-G-B-E

Swinging 8ths (♫ = ♩♪)

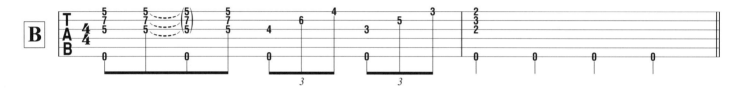

In 6ths:

Drop D tuning:
(low to high) D-A-D-G-B-E

Swinging 8ths (♫ = ♩♪)

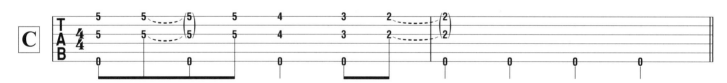

Drop D tuning:
(low to high) D-A-D-G-B-E

Swinging 8ths (♫ = ♩♪)

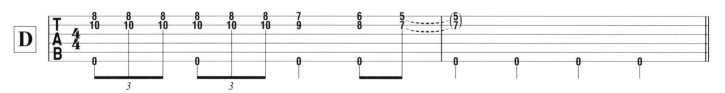

Drop D tuning:
(low to high) D-A-D-G-B-E

Swinging 8ths (♫ = ♩♪)

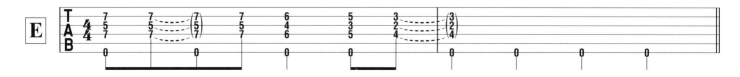

Drop D tuning:
(low to high) D-A-D-G-B-E

Swinging 8ths (♪♪ = ³♩♪)

F

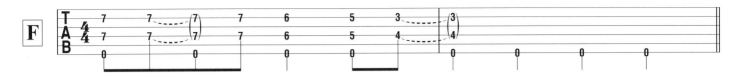

Drop D tuning:
(low to high) D-A-D-G-B-E

Swinging 8ths (♪♪ = ³♩♪)

G

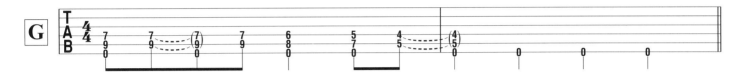

Of course, *every* key has these moveable elements but it's very hard, if not impossible, to play it with a steady bass in keys without an open bass string.

10.4. Solo in E with Moveable Modules ▶

Swinging 8ths (♪♪ = ³♩♪)

5

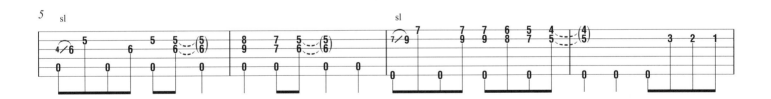

9

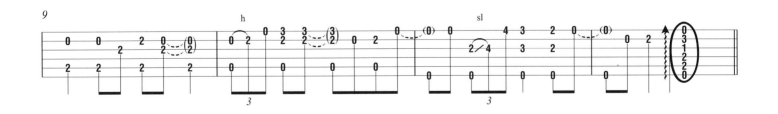

10.5. Solo in A with Moveable Modules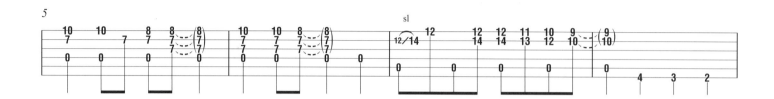

Swinging 8ths (♫ = ♩♪)

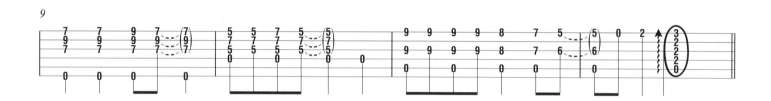

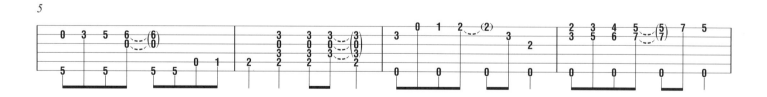

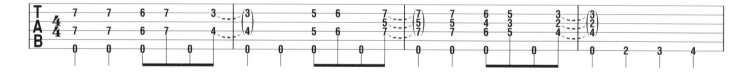

10.6. Solo in D with Moveable Modules

Dropped D Tuning (DADGBE)

Drop D tuning:
(low to high) D-A-D-G-B-E

Swinging 8ths (♫ = ♩♪)

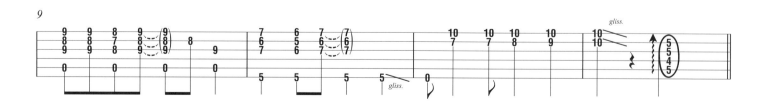

CHAPTER ELEVEN

11.1. Turnarounds in E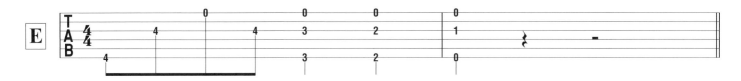

A typical module in blues music is the "turnaround." It usually starts in bar 11 of a 12-bar blues. Here's a little collection of E turnarounds. They can be played in both directions. I have only written them from high to low!

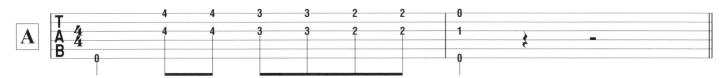

The same, but with a different rhythm:

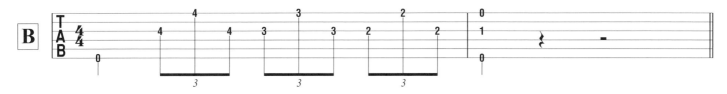

With additional notes on the 5th string:

A rather "modern" one:

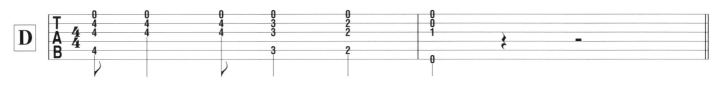

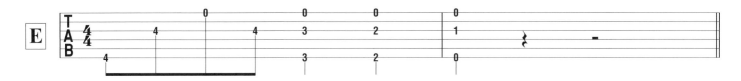

A "classy" one:

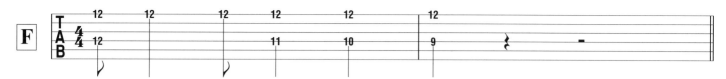

Swinging 8ths (♪♪ = ♪♪³)

Swinging 8ths (♪♪ = ♪♪³)

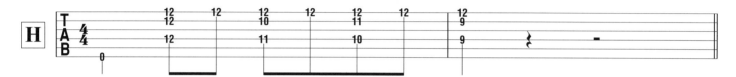

11.2. Turnarounds in A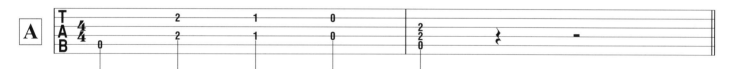

We know these next two from the "moveable modules!" Some of these can be used as turnarounds!

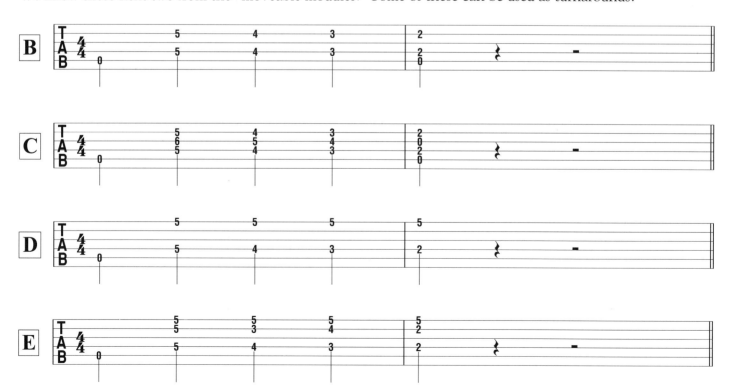

F

A "classy" one:

Swinging 8ths (♫ = ♩ ♪)

G

11.3. Turnarounds in D

Dropped D Tuning (DADGBE)

Drop D tuning:
(low to high) D-A-D-G-B-E

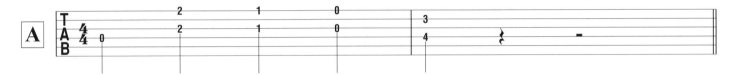

A

The same, but on different strings:

Drop D tuning:
(low to high) D-A-D-G-B-E

B

Drop D tuning:
(low to high) D-A-D-G-B-E

C

Drop D tuning:
(low to high) D-A-D-G-B-E

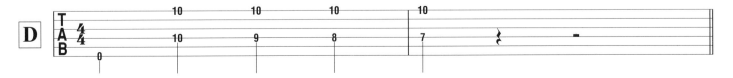

D

Drop D tuning:
(low to high) D-A-D-G-B-E

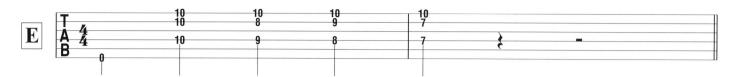

Drop D tuning:
(low to high) D-A-D-G-B-E

Drop D tuning:
(low to high) D-A-D-G-B-E

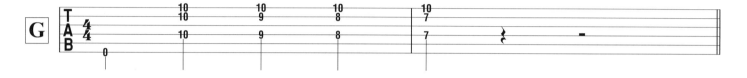

CHAPTER TWELVE

12.1. "Make Me a Pallet on Your Floor"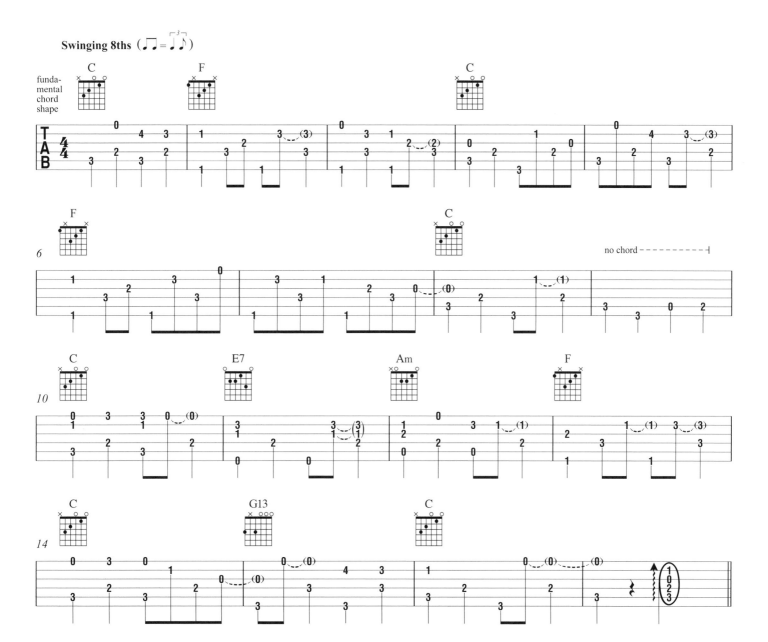

12.2. Discussion on "Make Me a Pallet on Your Floor"

As I have said before, we always have many possibilities to bring variety into our playing!

1. When we compare the sung melody and the chords of bars 1–8, we can easily hear that it's more or less the same, twice through. In our solo, however, I tried to vary bars 5–8. I mainly did that by playing the melody notes as syncopations.

How many of the melody notes should be played as syncopations is a matter of taste. For some, there are probably a few too many syncopations in this example, and they are perfectly correct in choosing to use less of them.

2. We could insert a further possible variation (in a second solo, for example) in bars 11 and 12 by using different chord positions and modifying the melody a little.

Variation for bars 11, 12, and 13:

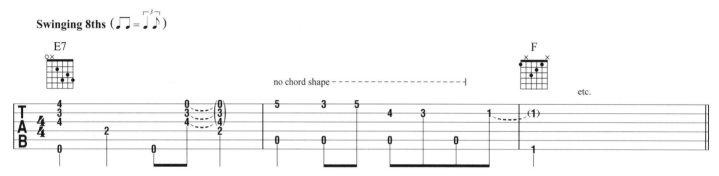

3. Bars 14 and 15 are arranged quite straight in rhythmic aspects. Let's add some syncopations, plus one downward slide in combination with a bass note!

Variation for bars 14 and 15:

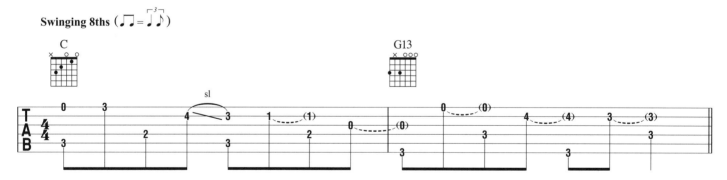

Of course, these are only a few possibilities to vary the arrangement. We always have to decide whether a variation fits the original song (again, a matter of taste) or not. We should always try to preserve the character of a song and we should never overdo it!

Here then is a modified version of "Make Me a Pallet on Your Floor":

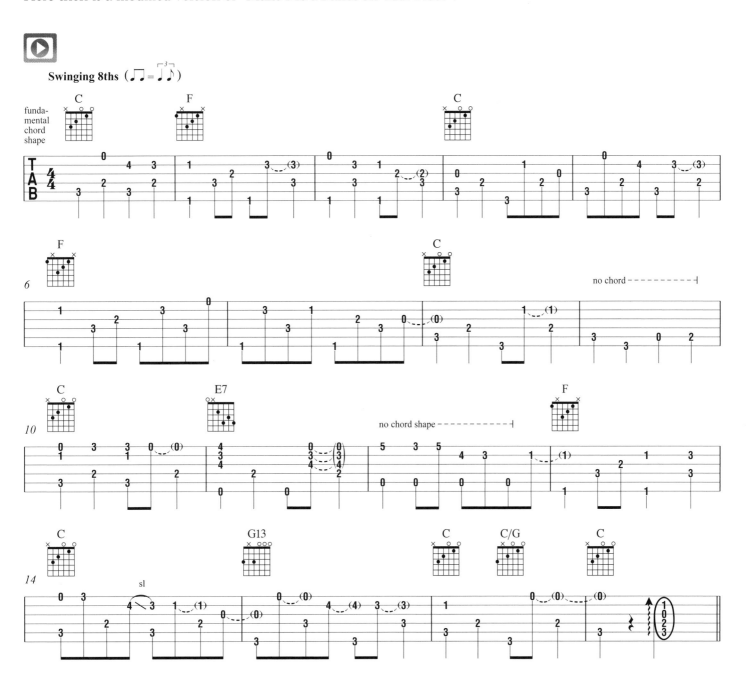

12.3. "What's the Matter with the Mill"

l usually play this one in the key of A, but let's have a look at an easier version in G!

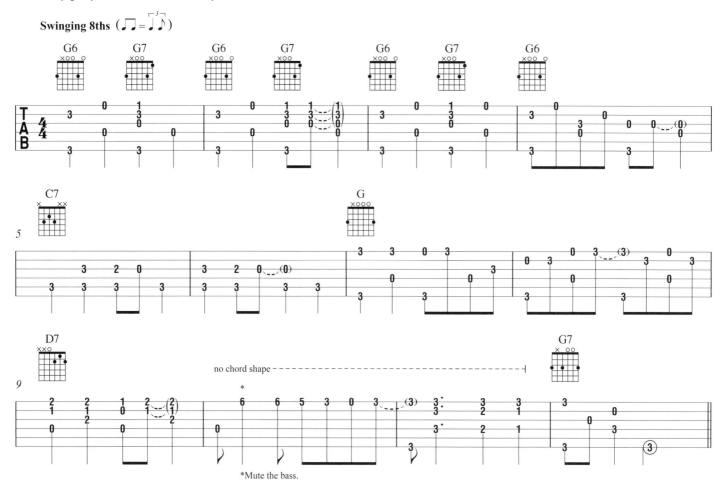

12.4. Discussion on "What's the Matter with the Mill"

1. To improve the first four bars, we should try to design the rhythm to be a little less static. So I added some syncopations in the first two bars and replaced the alternating, steady bass groove in bars 3 and 4 with a little solo lick instead. I also added a little bass line at the end as an approach to the next bass note (C).

Variation for bars 1–4:

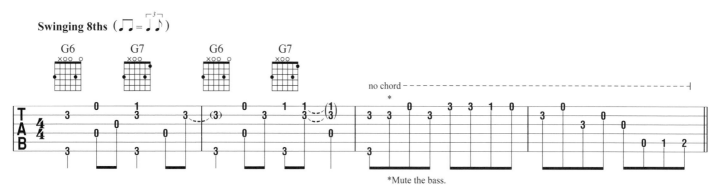

2. To play the melody of the next two bars one octave higher may be a little more elaborate, but in my opinion, it's worthwhile because this gives the melody more power. I also added a little bass line towards the next bass note (G) again.

Variation for bars 5 and 6:

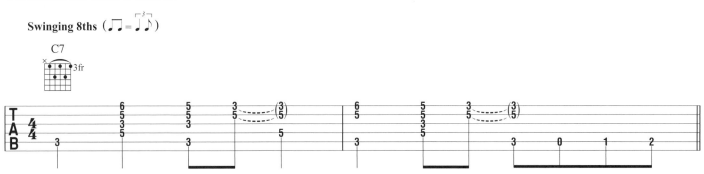

Here is the modified version of "What's the Matter with the Mill":

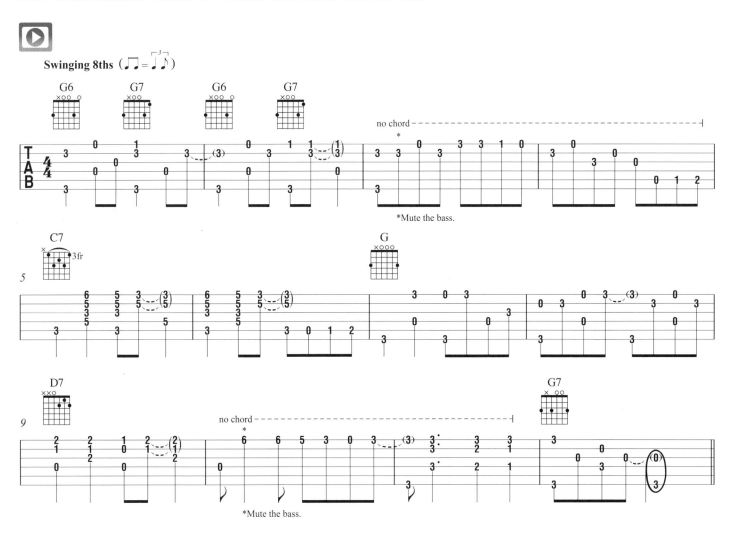

Rainer's Blues School Sign-Off

FINGERPICKING GUITAR BOOKS

Hone your fingerpicking skills with these great songbooks featuring solo guitar arrangements in standard notation and tablature. The arrangements in these books are carefully written for intermediate-level guitarists. Each song combines melody and harmony in one superb guitar fingerpicking arrangement. Each book also includes an introduction to basic fingerstyle guitar.

    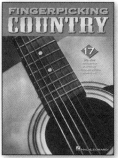 

Fingerpicking Acoustic
00699614 15 songs........................ $14.99

Fingerpicking Acoustic Classics
00160211 15 songs........................ $16.99

Fingerpicking Acoustic Hits
00160202 15 songs........................ $12.99

Fingerpicking Acoustic Rock
00699764 14 songs........................ $12.99

Fingerpicking Ballads
00699717 15 songs........................ $14.99

Fingerpicking Beatles
00699049 30 songs........................ $24.99

Fingerpicking Beethoven
00702390 15 pieces........................ $9.99

Fingerpicking Blues
00701277 15 songs $10.99

Fingerpicking Broadway Favorites
00699843 15 songs........................ $9.99

Fingerpicking Broadway Hits
00699838 15 songs........................ $7.99

Fingerpicking Campfire
00275964 15 songs........................ $12.99

Fingerpicking Celtic Folk
00701148 15 songs........................ $10.99

Fingerpicking Children's Songs
00699712 15 songs........................ $9.99

Fingerpicking Christian
00701076 15 songs........................ $12.99

Fingerpicking Christmas
00699599 20 carols........................ $10.99

Fingerpicking Christmas Classics
00701695 15 songs........................ $7.99

Fingerpicking Christmas Songs
00171333 15 songs........................ $10.99

Fingerpicking Classical
00699620 15 pieces........................ $10.99

Fingerpicking Country
00699687 17 songs........................ $12.99

Fingerpicking Disney
00699711 15 songs........................ $16.99

Fingerpicking Early Jazz Standards
00276565 15 songs $12.99

Fingerpicking Duke Ellington
00699845 15 songs........................ $9.99

Fingerpicking Enya
00701161 15 songs........................ $15.99

Fingerpicking Film Score Music
00160143 15 songs........................ $12.99

Fingerpicking Gospel
00701059 15 songs........................ $9.99

Fingerpicking Hit Songs
00160195 15 songs........................ $12.99

Fingerpicking Hymns
00699688 15 hymns $12.99

Fingerpicking Irish Songs
00701965 15 songs........................ $10.99

Fingerpicking Italian Songs
00159778 15 songs........................ $12.99

Fingerpicking Jazz Favorites
00699844 15 songs........................ $12.99

Fingerpicking Jazz Standards
00699840 15 songs........................ $10.99

Fingerpicking Elton John
00237495 15 songs........................ $14.99

Fingerpicking Latin Favorites
00699842 15 songs........................ $12.99

Fingerpicking Latin Standards
00699837 15 songs........................ $15.99

Fingerpicking Andrew Lloyd Webber
00699839 14 songs........................ $16.99

Fingerpicking Love Songs
00699841 15 songs........................ $14.99

Fingerpicking Love Standards
00699836 15 songs $9.99

Fingerpicking Lullabyes
00701276 16 songs........................ $9.99

Fingerpicking Movie Music
00699919 15 songs........................ $12.99

Fingerpicking Mozart
00699794 15 pieces........................ $9.99

Fingerpicking Pop
00699615 15 songs........................ $14.99

Fingerpicking Popular Hits
00139079 14 songs........................ $12.99

Fingerpicking Praise
00699714 15 songs........................ $12.99

Fingerpicking Rock
00699716 15 songs........................ $12.99

Fingerpicking Standards
00699613 17 songs........................ $14.99

Fingerpicking Wedding
00699637 15 songs........................ $10.99

Fingerpicking Worship
00700554 15 songs........................ $14.99

Fingerpicking Neil Young – Greatest Hits
00700134 16 songs........................ $14.99

Fingerpicking Yuletide
00699654 16 songs........................ $12.99

HAL•LEONARD®

Order these and more great publications from your favorite music retailer at
halleonard.com

Prices, contents and availability subject to change without notice.

 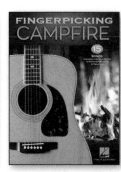    

MASTER THE *Blues*

BLUES GUITAR
Instruction Books from Hal Leonard

All books include notes & tablature

12-Bar Blues
by Dave Rubin

The term "12-bar blues" has become synonymous with blues music and is the basis for other forms of popular music. This book is devoted to providing guitarists with all the technical tools necessary for playing 12-bar blues with authority. Covers: boogie, shuffle, swing, riff, and jazzy blues progressions; Chicago, minor, slow, bebop, and other blues styles; soloing, intros, turnarounds, and more.
00695187 Book/Online Audio..............$19.99

75 Blues Turnarounds
by Michael DoCampo with Toby Wine

This book/audio pack teaches 75 turnarounds over common chord progressions in a variety of styles, including those of blues guitar greats like Albert King, Johnny Winter, Mike Bloomfield, Duane Allman, Jeff Beck, T-Bone Walker and others.
02501043 Book/Online Audio..............$12.99

100 Blues Lessons
Guitar Lesson Goldmine
by John Heussenstamm and Chad Johnson

A huge variety of blues guitar styles and techniques are covered, including: turnarounds, hammer-ons and pull-offs, slides, the blues scale, 12-bar blues, double stops, muting techniques, hybrid picking, fingerstyle blues, and much more!
00696452 Book/Online Audio..............$24.99

101 Must-Know Blues Licks
by Wolf Marshall

Now you can add authentic blues feel and flavor to your playing! Here are 101 definitive licks – plus a demonstration CD – from every major blues guitar style, neatly organized into easy-to-use categories. They're all here, including Delta blues, jump blues, country blues, Memphis blues, Texas blues, West Coast blues, Chicago blues, and British blues.
00695318 Book/Online Audio..............$19.99

Beginning Blues Guitar
by Dave Rubin

From B.B. King and Buddy Guy to Eric Clapton and Stevie Ray Vaughan, blues guitar is a constant in American popular music. This book teaches the concepts and techniques fostered by legendary blues guitar players: 12-bar blues; major & minor pentatonic scales; the blues scale; string bending; licks; double-stops; intros and turnarounds; and more.
00695916 Book/Online Audio..............$12.99

Beginning Fingerstyle Blues Guitar
by Arnie Berle & Mark Galbo

A step-by-step method for learning this rich and powerful style. Takes you from the fundamentals of fingerpicking to five authentic blues tunes. Includes graded exercises, illustrated tips, plus standard notation and tablature.
14003799 Book/CD Pack....................$22.99

Brave New Blues Guitar
by Greg Koch

A kaleidoscopic reinterpretation of 16 blues rock titans is the hallmark of this Greg Koch book with over three hours of online video lessons. It breaks down the styles, techniques, and licks of guitarists including Albert Collins, B.B. King, Eric Clapton, Jimi Hendrix, Stevie Ray Vaughan, Johnny Winter and more.
00201987 Book/Online Video.............$22.99

Chicago Blues Rhythm Guitar
by Bob Margolin & Dave Rubin

This definitive instructional guitar book features loads of rhythm guitar playing examples to learn and practice, covering a variety of styles, techniques, tips, historical anecdotes, and much more. To top it off, every playing example in the book is performed on the accompanying DVD by Bob Margolin himself!
00121575 Book/DVD Pack.................$22.99

Everything About Playing the Blues
by Wilbur Savidge

An ideal reference guide to playing the blues for all guitarists. Full instruction on blues theory, chords, rhythm, scales, advanced solo technique, beginnings and endings, riff construction and more. Includes play-along audio with 12 jam tracks.
14010625 Book/Online Audio...............$29.99

Fretboard Roadmaps – Blues Guitar
by Fred Sokolow

Fretboard patterns are roadmaps that all great blues guitarists know and use. This book teaches how to: play lead and rhythm anywhere on the fretboard; play a variety of lead guitar styles; play chords and progressions anywhere on the fretboard, in any key; expand chord vocabulary; learn to think musically, the way the pros do.
00695350 Book/Online Audio..............$15.99

Hal Leonard Blues Guitar Method
by Greg Koch

Real blues songs are used to teach the basics of rhythm and lead blues guitar in the style of B.B. King, Buddy Guy, Eric Clapton, and many others. Lessons include: 12-bar blues; chords, scales and licks; vibrato and string bending; riffs, turnarounds, and boogie patterns; and more!
00697326 Book/Online Audio..............$19.99

How to Play Blues-Fusion Guitar
by Joe Charupakorn

Study the scales, chords, and arpeggios most commonly used in the blues-fusion style and how to use them in this book. You'll also examine how artists like Matt Schofield, Mike Stern, Scott Henderson, and John Scofield put their own spin on the blues/fusion format.
00137813 Book/Online Audio..............$19.99

Blues You Can Use Series
by John Ganapes

Blues You Can Use
This comprehensive source for learning blues guitar is designed to develop both your lead and rhythm playing. Blues styles covered include Texas, Delta, R&B, early rock & roll, gospel and blues/rock.
00142420 Book/Online Media..........................$22.99

More Blues You Can Use
This follow up edition covers: pentatonic scales, single-note tremolo, double-string bends, reverse bends, shuffle rhythms, 6th and 9th chords, boogie patterns, chord substitutions, vibrato techniques, and more!
00695165 Book/Online Audio.........................$22.99

Blues Guitar Chords You Can Use
A reference guide to blues, R&B, jazz, and rock rhythm guitar, with hundreds of voicings, chord theory construction, chord progressions and exercises and much more.
00695082...$17.99

Blues Licks You Can Use
Contains music and performance notes for 75 hot lead phrases, covering styles including up-tempo and slow blues, jazz-blues, shuffle blues, swing blues and more!
00695386 Book/Online Audio $17.99

Blues Rhythms You Can Use
Develop your rhythm playing chops with 21 progressive lessons: basic rhythm theory; major and minor blues; 8th, 16th and triplets; extensions; passing chords; lead-rhythm style; funky blues; jump blues; blues rock; and more.
00696038 Book/Online Audio $22.99

HAL•LEONARD®

Order these and more publications from your favorite music retailer at halleonard.com

1221
312

Prices, availability, and contents subject to change without notice.

HAL•LEONARD
BLUES PLAY-ALONG

For use with all the C, B♭, Bass Clef and E♭ Instruments, the Hal Leonard Blues Play-Along Series is the ultimate jamming tool for all blues musicians.

With easy-to-read lead sheets, and other split-track choices, these first-of-a-kind packages will bring your local blues jam right into your house! Each song includes two tracks: a full stereo mix, and a split track mix with removable guitar, bass, piano, and harp parts. The CD is playable on any CD player, and is also enhanced so Mac and PC users can adjust the recording to any tempo without changing the pitch!

1. Chicago Blues
All Your Love (I Miss Loving) • Easy Baby • I Ain't Got You • I'm Your Hoochie Coochie Man • Killing Floor • Mary Had a Little Lamb • Messin' with the Kid • Sweet Home Chicago.
00843106 Book/CD Pack $17.99

2. Texas Blues
Hide Away • If You Love Me Like You Say • Mojo Hand • Okie Dokie Stomp • Pride and Joy • Reconsider Baby • T-Bone Shuffle • The Things That I Used to Do.
00843107 Book/CD Pack $12.99

3. Slow Blues
Don't Throw Your Love on Me So Strong • Five Long Years • I Can't Quit You Baby • I Just Want to Make Love to You • The Sky Is Crying • (They Call It) Stormy Monday (Stormy Monday Blues) • Sweet Little Angel • Texas Flood.
00843108 Book/CD Pack $12.99

4. Shuffle Blues
Beautician Blues • Bright Lights, Big City • Further on up the Road • I'm Tore Down • Juke • Let Me Love You Baby • Look at Little Sister • Rock Me Baby.
00843171 Book/CD Pack $12.99

5. B.B. King
Everyday I Have the Blues • It's My Own Fault Darlin' • Just Like a Woman • Please Accept My Love • Sweet Sixteen • The Thrill Is Gone • Why I Sing the Blues • You Upset Me Baby.
00843172 Book/CD Pack $14.99

7. Howlin' Wolf
Built for Comfort • Forty-Four • How Many More Years • Killing Floor • Moanin' at Midnight • Shake for Me • Sitting on Top of the World • Smokestack Lightning.
00843176 Book/CD Pack $12.99

8. Blues Classics
Baby, Please Don't Go • Boom Boom • Born Under a Bad Sign • Dust My Broom • How Long, How Long Blues • I Ain't Superstitious • It Hurts Me Too • My Babe.
00843177 Book/CD Pack $12.99

9. Albert Collins
Brick • Collins' Mix • Don't Lose Your Cool • Frost Bite • Frosty • I Ain't Drunk • Master Charge • Trash Talkin'.
00843178 Book/CD Pack $12.99

10. Uptempo Blues
Cross Road Blues (Crossroads) • Give Me Back My Wig • Got My Mo Jo Working • The House Is Rockin' • Paying the Cost to Be the Boss • Rollin' and Tumblin' • Turn on Your Love Light • You Can't Judge a Book by the Cover.
00843179 Book/CD Pack $12.99

11. Christmas Blues
Back Door Santa • Blue Christmas • Dig That Crazy Santa Claus • Merry Christmas, Baby • Please Come Home for Christmas • Santa Baby • Soulful Christmas.
00843203 Book/CD Pack $12.99

12. Jimmy Reed
Ain't That Lovin' You Baby • Baby, What You Want Me to Do • Big Boss Man • Bright Lights, Big City • Going to New York • Honest I Do • You Don't Have to Go • You Got Me Dizzy.
00843204 Book/CD Pack $12.99

13. Blues Standards
Ain't Nobody's Business • Kansas City • Key to the Highway • Let the Good Times Roll • Night Time Is the Right Time • Route 66 • See See Rider • Stormy Weather (Keeps Rainin' All the Time).
00843205 Book/CD Pack $12.99

14. Muddy Waters
Good Morning Little Schoolgirl • Honey Bee • I Can't Be Satisfied • I'm Ready • Mannish Boy • Rollin' Stone (Catfish Blues) • Trouble No More (Someday Baby) • You Shook Me.
00843206 Book/CD Pack $12.99

15. Blues Ballads
Ain't No Sunshine • As the Years Go Passing By • Darlin' You Know I Love You • Have You Ever Loved a Woman • I'd Rather Go Blind • Somebody Loan Me a Dime • Third Degree • Three Hours past Midnight.
00843207 Book/CD Pack $14.99

17. Stevie Ray Vaughan
Ain't Gone 'n' Give up on Love • Couldn't Stand the Weather • Crossfire • Empty Arms • Honey Bee • Love Struck Baby • Rude Mood • Scuttle Buttin'.
00843214 Book/Audio $14.99

18. Jimi Hendrix
Fire • Foxey Lady • Jam 292 • Little Wing • Red House • Spanish Castle Magic • Voodoo Child (Slight Return) • Who Knows.
00843218 Book/CD Pack $14.99

HAL•LEONARD®

www.halleonard.com